WRECK THIS
JOURNAL
EVERYWHERE

TO CREATE IS TO DESTROY

BY KERI SMITH

A PERIGEE BOOK

A PERIGEE BOOK
PUBLISHED BY THE PENGUIN GROUP
PENGUIN GROUP (USA) LLC
375 HUDSON STREET, NEW YORK, NEW YORK 10014

USA • CANADA • UK • IRELAND • AUSTRALIA • NEW ZEALAND • INDIA • SOUTH AFRICA • CHINA

PENGUIN.COM

A PENGUIN RANDOM HOUSE COMPANY

WRECK THIS JOURNAL EVERYWHERE

ISBN: 978-0-399-17191-8

FIRST EDITION: JUNE 2014
PORTIONS OF THIS BOOK PREVIOUSLY APPEARED IN THE EXPANDED EDITION OF
WRECK THIS JOURNAL BY KERI SMITH, PUBLISHED BY PERIGEE IN AUGUST 2012.

PRINTED IN THE UNITED STATES OF AMERICA

10 9 8 7 6 5 4 3 2 1

ART AND DESIGN BY KERI SMITH

WARNING: DURING THE PROCESS OF THIS BOOK YOU WILL GET DIRTY. YOU MAY FIND YOURSELF COVERED IN PAINT, OR ANY OTHER NUMBER OF FOREIGN SUBSTANCES. YOU WILL GET WET. YOU MAY BE ASKED TO DO THINGS YOU QUESTION. YOU MAY GRIEVE FOR THE PERFECT STATE THAT YOU FOUND THE BOOK IN. YOU MAY BEGIN TO SEE CREATIVE DESTRUCTION EVERYWHERE. YOU MAY BEGIN TO LIVE MORE RECKLESSLY.

DEAR READER/USER,
THIS VERSION OF <u>WRECK THIS JOURNAL</u>
WAS MADE TO BE USED WHILE YOU
ARE OUT IN THE WORLD, (HENCE
ITS PORTABLE SIZE).
IT HAS SOME NEW PROMPTS
SPECIFIC TO THE OUTDOORS
BUT ALSO CONTAINS SOME
OF YOUR OLD FAVORITES.
SO STOP READING THIS AND
GO OUTSIDE! TIME TO
START A NEW ADVENTURE.
HAPPY WRECKING.
SINCERELY YOURS,
    KERI SMITH

1. Carry this with you everywhere you go.
2. Follow the instructions on every page.
3. Order is not important.
4. Instructions are open to interpretation.
5. Experiment.
(work against your better judgment.)

materials

ideas
gum
glue
dirt
saliva
water
weather
garbage
plant life
pencil/pen
needle & thread
stamps
stickers
sticky things
sticks
spoons
comb
twist tie
ink
paint
grass
detergent
grease
tears
crayons

smells
hands
string
ball
unpredictability
spontaneity
photos
newspaper
white things
office supplies
wax
found items
stapler
food
tea/coffee
emotions
fears
shoes
matches
biology
scissors
tape
time
happenstance
gumption
sharp things

ADD YOUR OWN PAGE NUMBERS.

STARTING HERE

DEVISE A
WAY TO
CARRY
THE
JOURNAL
EVERYWHERE.

ACQUIRE A NAPKIN FROM
A RESTAURANT. WRITE
A SECRET ON IT.
GLUE IT HERE.

MAKE A MARK EVERY TIME YOU SPOT A BIRD.

CHOOSE YOUR OWN

WRECKING METHOD ⬆

SIGN   DATE

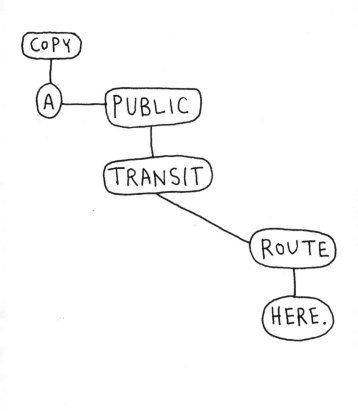

COPY
A — PUBLIC
TRANSIT
ROUTE
HERE.

HIDE PARTS
OF THIS PAGE
ON YOUR
TRAVELS.

POKE HOLES IN
THIS PAGE USING
SOMETHING YOU FIND
ON YOUR TRAVELS.

FLOAT THIS PAGE.

← root beer

USE THIS SPACE WHILE DREAMING OUTSIDE.

DRAW SOMETHING BASED ON THE

MOON

●	FULL	DRAW WHAT IS ABOVE YOU.
☾	WAXING	DRAW WHAT IS TO YOUR LEFT.
☽	WANING	DRAW WHAT IS TO YOUR RIGHT.

RUB HERE WITH DIRT.

COVER THIS
PAGE WITH
ODD THINGS
YOU FIND.

DRAW
SOMETHING
HERE

 WITH A PEN.

GO OUT IN THE

RAIN OR SNOW.

LET IT GET WET.

COLLECT NUMBERS

FROM THE WORLD HERE.

compost this page.

watch it deteriorate.

CHOOSE YOUR OWN

WRECKING
METHOD ⬆

SIGN   DATE

DOCUMENT TIME PASSING IN A NEW ENVIRONMENT.

HIDE THIS PAGE IN SOMEONE'S POCKET OR BAG WITH A NOTE.

CLIMB
UP HIGH
DROP THE
JOURNAL.

FIND A PIECE
OF CARDBOARD
IN THE NEXT
FIVE MINUTES.
TAPE IT
HERE.

WRITE LITTLE NOTES
TO TEAR OUT AND LEAVE
FOR OTHERS (IN PUBLIC).

WRITE DOWN ALL THE

STREET NAMES

IN YOUR IMMEDIATE VICINITY.

GO FOR A WALK, DRAG IT.

TIE A STRING TO THE JOURNAL.

GET THIS PAGE
STAMPED BY
SOMEONE.
(HINT: TRY THE POST
OFFICE.)

CHOOSE YOUR OWN

WRECKING
METHOD ⬆

_____

_____

SIGN   DATE

COVER THIS PAGE IN CIRCLES THAT YOU FIND

draw lines
ON THE BUS, ON A

While IN MOTION,
TRAIN, WHILE WALKING.

DROP MUD HERE. REPEAT.

TAKE A WALK. DRAW YOUR PATH HERE.

Infuse this
page with a
smell of your
choosing.

PLACE THIS PAGE
FACEDOWN ON
THE GROUND AND
KICK IT AROUND
FOR A WHILE.

CHOOSE YOUR OWN

WRECKING METHOD ⬆

SIGN   DATE

FIND TEN VERY SMALL ITEMS TO GLUE HERE WHILE GOING ABOUT YOUR BUSINESS.

COVER THIS PAGE

USING ONLY ITEMS FOUND
IN THE OUTDOORS.

TRACE THINGS FROM OUTSIDE. LET THE LINES OVERLAP.

SMUSH
SOMETHING
COLORFUL
ONTO THIS
PAGE.

COVER THIS
PAGE IN LINES
THAT YOU FIND.

WHILE YOU ARE OUT FOR A WALK, SCRAPE THIS PAGE ON A VARIETY OF NATURAL SURFACES AS YOU GO.

CHOOSE YOUR OWN

WRECKING
METHOD ⬆

SIGN   DATE

COLLECT
DEAD
BUGS
HERE.

WORDS

FILL THE ENTIRE PAGE WITH
YOU SEE ON YOUR ADVENTURES.

TURN THIS PAGE BLACK*

*USING ITEMS FOUND IN THE WORLD.

THIS PAGE IS A
WORK IN PROGRESS.
(ADD SOMETHING
FROM EVERY
ENVIRONMENT YOU
VISIT IN A DAY.)

ROLL THE JOURNAL DOWN A LARGE HILL.

COVER THIS PAGE WITH VERY TINY THOUGHTS FROM EVERYWHERE.

Wacthing movie

DO SOME LEAF PRINTS.

FIND A GREEN LEAF.
FIND A ROCK.
TURN PAGE OVER.
HAMMER THE SPOT
WHERE THE LEAF
IS USING THE ROCK.

FIND A WAY TO WEAR THE JOURNAL.

CHOOSE YOUR OWN

WRECKING
METHOD ⬆

SIGN   DATE

find a piece of string.

TIE THIS PAGE UP WITH IT.

TAKE A WALK.
THEN STAND HERE.

(WIPE YOUR FEET, JUMP UP AND DOWN.)

HANG THE JOURNAL IN A PUBLIC PLACE.
INVITE PEOPLE TO DRAW HERE.

USE THIS PLACE
FOR BLADES OF
GRASS YOU FIND.

COLLECT
names, AUTOGRAPHS, OTHER PEOPLE'S DREAMS.

CHOOSE YOUR OWN

WRECKING
METHOD ⬆

SIGN   DATE

WHILE WAITING FOR SOMETHING (FOOD, A PLANE, YOUR FRIEND TO ARRIVE), WRITE A LIST OF EVERYTHING YOU CAN SEE.

DIP THIS PAGE IN THREE DIFFERENT
SUBSTANCES FROM THREE DIFFERENT
ENVIRONMENTS

CUT OUT THESE BADGES.
LEAVE THEM IN A PUBLIC
PLACE FOR OTHER PEOPLE
TO WRECK.

THIS PAGE IS FOR HANDPRINTS OR FINGERPRINTS.
GET THEM DIRTY THEN PRESS DOWN.

CHOOSE YOUR OWN

WRECKING
METHOD ⬆

_____

SIGN   DATE

STAIN LOG

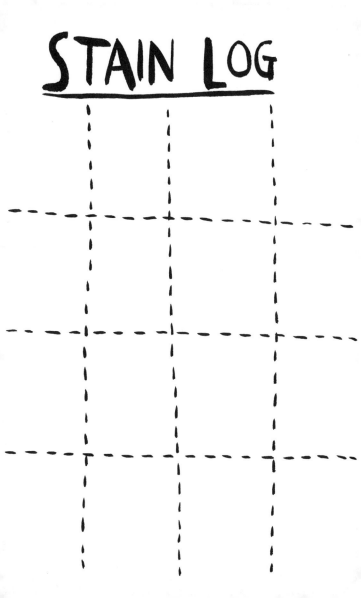

WRECKING LOCATION LOG

DRAW A MAP AND LOG EVERYWHERE THAT YOU'VE WRECKED.

ACKNOWLEDGMENTS

THIS BOOK WAS MADE WITH THE HELP OF THE FOLLOWING PEOPLE: JEFFERSON PITCHER, STEVE LAMBERT, CYNTHIA YARDLEY, MEG LEDER, FAITH HAMLIN, CORITA KENT, JOHN CAGE, ROSS MENDES, BRENDA UELAND, BRUNO MUNARI, CHARLES AND RAE EAMES, AND GEORGES PEREC. DEDICATED TO PERFECTIONISTS ALL OVER THE WORLD.

KERI SMITH IS AN AGENT FOR A SECRET UNDERGROUND ORGANIZATION WHOSE MISSION IS TO REANIMATE EVERYDAY LIFE AND QUESTION THE STATUS QUO. SHE SPENDS HER TIME CONDUCTING HER "RESEARCH" UP IN TREES WATCHING THE WORLD AND TAKING DETAILED NOTES. SHE USES HER FINDINGS TO CREATE BOOKS AND CONCEPTUAL ARTWORKS. YOU CAN FIND SOME OF HER RESEARCH AT KERISMITH.COM.

WHERE WILL YOU WRECK?
#WRECKEVERYWHERE

ALSO FROM KERI SMITH

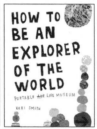

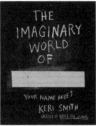

PENGUIN.COM/KERISMITH
KERISMITH.COM
KERISMITHBOOKS.TUMBLR.COM
TWITTER.COM/WRECKTHISTWIT

 PERIGEE

T401-0314